A Kid's Guide to Learning French

A Children's Learn French Books

BABY PROFESSOR

EDUCATION KIDS

Nombres
(Numbers)

Un

[uh(n)]

one

Deux

[duh]

two

Trois

[trwah]

three

Quatre

[kahtr]

four

Cinq

[sa(n)k]

five

Six

[sees]

six

Sept

[seht]

seven

Huit

[weet]

eight

Neuf

[nuhf]

nine

Neuf Neuf

Neuf Neuf

Neuf Neuf

Dix

[dees]

ten

Onze

[oh(n)z]
eleven

Douze

[dooz]

twelve

Treize

[*trehz*]

thirteen

Quatorze

[kah-tohrz]

fourteen

Quinze

[ka(n)z]

fifteen

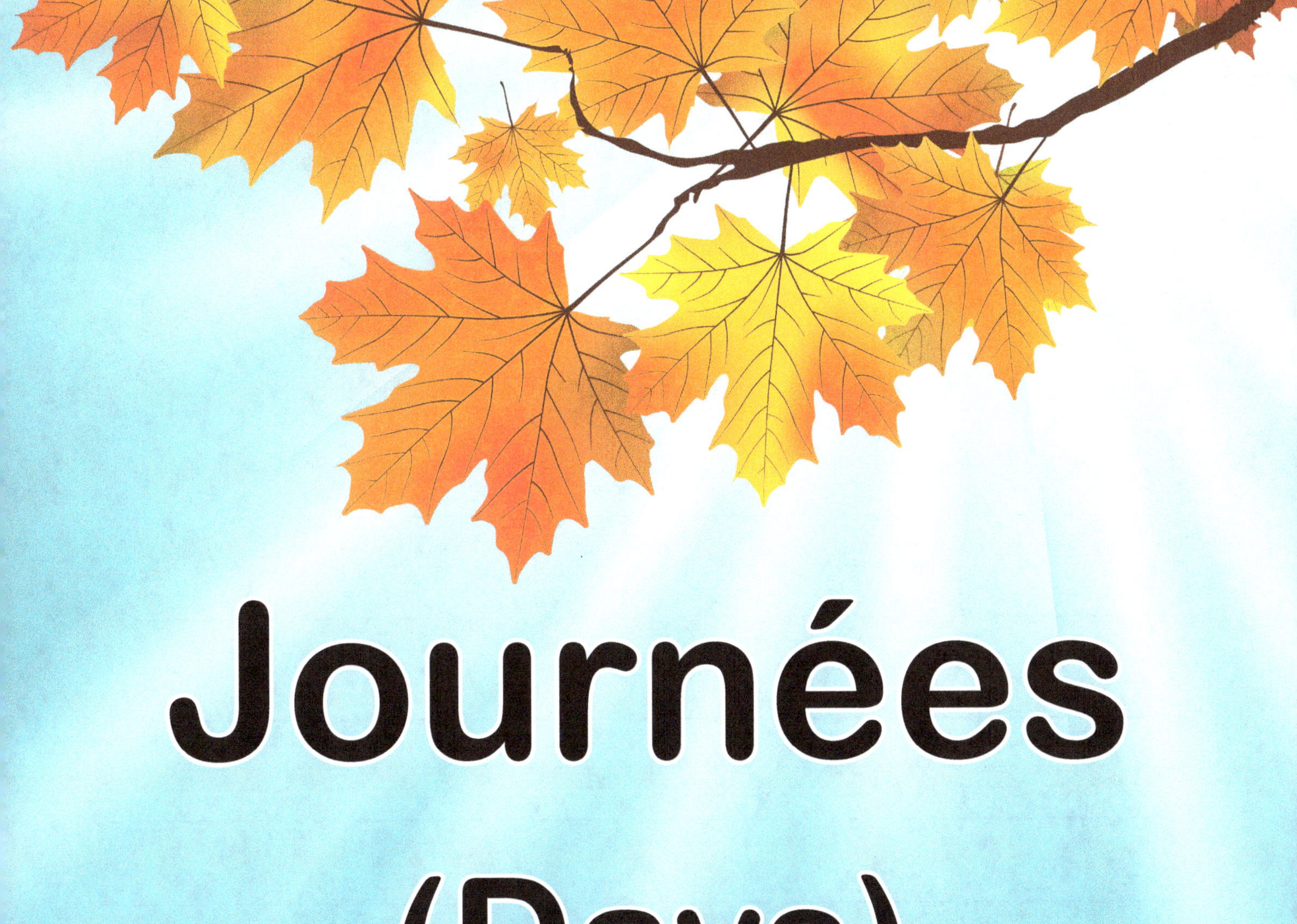

Journées
(Days)

Lundi

luh(n)-dee

Monday

Mardi

mahr-dee

Tuesday

Mercredi

mehr-kruh-dee

Wednesday

Jeudi

zhuh-dee

Thursday

Vendredi

vah(n)-druh-dee

Friday

Samedi

sahm-dee

Saturday

Dimanche

dee-mah(n)sh

Sunday

Months

(Mois)

Janvier

zhah(n)-vyay

January

Février

fay-vree-yay

February

Mars

mahrs

March

Avril

ah-vreel

April

Mai

meh

May

Juin

zhwa(n)

June

Juillet

zhwee-eh

July

Août

oo or oot

August

Septembre

sehp-tah(n)br

September

Octobre

ohk-tohbr

October

Novembre

noh-vah(n)br
November

Décembre

day-sah(n)br

December

Visit

BABY PROFESSOR
EDUCATION KIDS

www.BabyProfessorBooks.com

to download Free Baby Professor eBooks
and view our catalog of new and exciting
Children's Books